Restoration
The Bride / The Wife

Apostle Andrea Lewis

Selah Communications, Inc.

Copyright © 2015 by Apostle Andrea Lewis.

All rights reserved.

No part of this book may be reproduced or transmitted in any form or by any means whatsoever: electronic or mechanical, including photocopying, recording, or by any information storage and retrieval system, etc., without permission in writing from the copyright owner.

All Scriptures are from the KJV.

Selah Communications, Inc.
PO Box 79493
Atlanta, GA 30357

Library of Congress Control Number: 2015957109

ISBN: 978-0-9909449-3-5 (Hardcover)
ISBN: 978-0-9909449-4-2 (E-Book)
ISBN: 978-0-9909449-5-9 (Paperback)

10 9 8 7 6 5 4 3 2 **1**

Dedication

To Judah (spiritual Israel, called and borne of Me) and Jerusalem (Israel, My chosen), from the Lord your God that loves you:

Hear, O heavens, and give ear, O earth: for the Lord hath spoken, I have nourished and brought up children, and they have rebelled against Me. The ox knoweth his owner, and the ass his master's crib: but Israel doth not know, My people doth not consider. Ah sinful nation, a people laden with iniquity, a seed of evildoers, children that are corrupters: they have forsaken the Lord, they have provoked the Holy One of Israel unto anger, they are gone away backward. Why should ye be stricken anymore? Ye will revolt more and more: the whole head is sick, and the whole heart faint. From the sole of the foot even unto the head there is no soundness in it; but wounds, and bruises, and putrifying sores: they have not been closed, neither bound up, neither mollified with ointment. Your country is desolate, your cities are burned with fire: your land, strangers devour it in your presence, and it is desolate, as overthrown by strangers. And the daughter of Zion is left as a cottage in a vineyard, as a lodge in a garden of cucumbers, as a besieged city. Except the Lord of hosts had left unto us a very small remnant, we should have been as Sodom, and we should have been like unto Gomorrah. Hear the Word of the Lord, ye rulers of Sodom; give ear unto the Law of our God, ye people of Gomorrah. To what purpose is the multitude of your sacrifices unto Me? Saith the Lord: I am full of the burnt offerings of rams, and the fat of fed beasts; and I delight not in the blood of bullocks, or of lambs, or of he goats. When ye come to appear before Me, who hath required this at your hand, to tread My courts? Bring no more vain oblations; incense is an abomination unto Me; the new moons and Sabbaths, the calling of assemblies, I cannot away with; it is iniquity, even the solemn

Restoration

meeting. Your new moons and your appointed feasts My soul hateth: they are a trouble unto Me; I am weary to bear them. And when ye spread forth your hands, I will hide Mine eyes from you: yea, when ye make many prayers, I will not hear: your hands are full of blood. Wash you, make you clean; put away the evil of your doings from before Mine eyes; cease to do evil; Learn to do well; seek judgment, relieve the oppressed, judge the fatherless, plead for the widow. Come now, and let us reason together, saith the Lord: though your sins be as scarlet, they shall be as white as snow; though they be red like crimson, they shall be as wool. If ye be willing and obedient, ye shall eat the good of the land: But if ye refuse and rebel, ye shall be devoured with the sword: for the mouth of the Lord hath spoken it. How is the faithful city become an harlot! It was full of judgment; righteousness lodged in it; but now murderers. Thy silver is become dross, thy wine mixed with water: Thy princes are rebellious, and companions of thieves: every one loveth gifts, and followeth after rewards: they judge not the fatherless, neither doth the cause of the widow come unto them. Therefore saith the Lord, the Lord of hosts, the Mighty One of Israel, Ah, I will ease Me of Mine adversaries, and avenge Me of Mine enemies: And I will turn My hand upon thee, and purely purge away thy dross, and take away all thy tin: And I will restore thy judges as at the first, and thy counselors as at the beginning: afterward thou shalt be called, The city of righteousness, the faithful city. Zion shall be redeemed with judgment, and her converts with righteousness. And the destruction of the transgressors and the sinners shall be together, and they that forsake the Lord shall be consumed. For they shall be ashamed of the oaks which ye have desired, and ye shall be confounded for the gardens that ye have chosen. For ye shall be as an oak whose leaf fadeth, and as a garden that hath no water. And the strong shall be as tow, and the maker of it as a spark, and they shall both burn together, and none shall quench them.

Table of Contents

Acknowledgment 7

Preface 9

Section I: Live 13

Section II: Stand 33

Section III: Virtue 45

Postface 57

Encouragement 59

Acknowledgment

Thank You, Jesus, for Your mercy on us. Thank You, Jesus, for Your grace toward us. Thank You, Jesus, for Your faithfulness toward us. Thank You, Jesus, for Your love for us. Thank You, Jesus, for Your heart toward the wholeness of the family and their oneness in You. Thank You, Jesus, for Your counsel on true intimacy, wholeness, and oneness in the relationship of marriage. Thank You, Jesus, for Your concern of the woman. Thank You, Jesus, for teaching the women how to be Your children of Light, Your bride: a pruned and nourished branch in Your body that will produce much good fruit. May the women surrender to You and obey so that You may complete that good work You started, that Your glory will be seen.

Preface

To the women of God:
Jesus is speaking to you with great love. Heed His counsel and surrender, so that you will be made firm in Him, as He desires, and that you may gain and maintain the intimacy He desires between you and Him.

Wives: Surrender to Jesus and His counsel that He may restore and make firm the intimacy that ought to be between you and your husband in the marriage created by Him.

Women who will marry: Surrender to Jesus and His counsel that He may prepare you and make you ready.

Why should you possess and live these instructions? Because it is the desire of Jesus that you be restored now; it is time, if you are willing and obedient. What will the result be should you obey His words? Restoration as His bride (godly, righteous, and whole women of His body/His Church). Restoration as the wife He has made as a help meet (fit and suitable) for the man (the godly servant and head) He has given you to. Restoration of full and complete intimacy between you and Jesus and between you and your husband as one flesh. Restoration of order to your household with God as the head and your husband in authority under God, fulfilling his duty to you and to the household as is pleasing to God, that you may all dwell intact and in peace. The restoration of all blessings He desires at this time that are promised, already

Restoration

revealed, and yet hidden. Only Jesus knows all that He desires we should have at this time, and He wants to release it now, if we are willing and obey Him. Receive it, in Jesus' name.

Restoration
The Bride / The Wife

Restoration: *to turn, to bring back, to build again, to set right, to make ready, to make new again, to reinstate, to re-establish, to make firm again; to return to former condition, place, and owner.*

Section I

Live

Ye mountains of Israel, hear the Word of the Lord God; Thus saith the Lord God to the mountains, and to the hills, to the rivers, and to the valleys; Behold, I, even I, will bring a sword upon you, and I will destroy your high places. And your altars shall be desolate, and your images shall be broken: and I will cast down your slain men before your idols. And I will lay the dead carcases of the children of Israel before their idols; and I will scatter your bones round about your altars. In all your dwelling places the cities shall be laid waste, and the high places shall be desolate; that your altars may be laid waste and made desolate, and your idols may be broken and cease, and your images may be cut down, and your works may be abolished. And the slain shall fall in the midst of you, and ye shall know that I am the Lord. Yet will I leave a remnant, that ye may have some that shall escape the sword among the nations, when ye shall be scattered through the countries. And they that escape of you shall remember Me among the nations whither they shall be carried captives, because I am broken with their whorish heart, which hath departed from Me, and with their eyes, which go a whoring after their idols: and they shall lothe themselves for the evils which they have committed in all their abominations. And they shall know that I am the Lord, and that I have not said in vain that I would do this evil unto them. Thus saith the Lord God; Smite with thine hand, and stamp with thy foot, and say, Alas for all the evil abominations of the house of Israel! for they shall fall by the sword, by the famine, and by the pestilence. He that is far off shall die of the pestilence; and he that is near shall fall by the sword; and he that remaineth and is besieged shall die by the famine: thus will I accomplish My fury upon them. Then shall ye know that I am the Lord, when their slain men shall be among their idols round about their altars, upon every high hill,

Restoration

in all the tops of the mountains, and under every green tree, and under every thick oak, the place where they did offer sweet savour to all their idols. So will I stretch out My hand upon them, and make the land desolate, yea, more desolate than the wilderness toward Diblath, in all their habitations: and they shall know that I am the Lord.

- **Sanctify God:** Declare (make clear) God as holy by revealing yourself as who He made you to be: the bride of Christ first. Let Christ be seen in you; be morally and spiritually excellent.
- ***Appearance***: Look well to (make sure of) the way you present yourself (within and without), because it reflects on Jesus and on your husband. Be in all manner presentable and upright before God and man.
- ***Behavior:*** Look well to (make sure of) the way you carry/conduct yourself; let Christ shine from within you, because it all reflects on Jesus and on your husband. Be in all manner presentable and upright before God and man.

Keep judgement: Abide in Jesus; possess discernment and good sense.
&
Do justice: Abide in Jesus; use and perform fairness.
(Then will)
Salvation come: Abide in Jesus; protection will occur (run to meet you/run against harm).
&
Righteousness be revealed: Abide in Jesus; morality will be exposed (set in place) and Jesus will be unveiled/seen.

Wisdom

Let it enter your heart; it will cause you to receive glory. Regard Jesus with reverence and awe, use good judgement; acknowledge Him always in everything you think, do, and feel. You have already been prepared; remember all you have received.

Live

Knowledge
Let it be pleasant to your soul. Be aware in all things; nothing is new. If there is a problem, do not be affected nor offended; you have already been prepared and are already victorious, because Jesus is with you. Have peace; speak and perform in a peaceful manner. You have already been prepared; remember all you have received.

Understanding
It is a wellspring of life to you if you possess it. It will keep you in a righteous path, deliver you from the way of evil and froward (contrary) things, deliver you from those who never knew Jesus, and deliver you from the paths of death. Use perception and apply good sense in all situations and circumstances. You have already been prepared; remember all you have received.

Fear
Jesus: Regard God with reverence (great and deep respect) and stand in awe of Him and His works. He is holy, true, faithful, and He loves you; honor Him, as you ought to.

Your husband: Regard your husband with deep respect and honor him, as you ought to. He was given with authority over you to be faithful and true, to love and care for you, and to be good to you.

Applied
Bride: Think of Jesus first and acknowledge Him in everything (in times of blessing and in times of trial). Nothing happens by chance or luck; all are by the will, desire, intention, allowance, and hand of God. Don't be moved, disturbed, anxious, or turned from serving Him but know that He is in full control and able of all things seen and unseen.

Wife: Think of your husband before yourself and before any other person or thing and acknowledge him in everything he does; he is strong, but he still

Restoration

needs you for support (emotional and physical), and that is why you were brought forth and given to him; it is your duty.

Righteousness

(If you possess it, Jesus will reveal His secrets to you.)

Jesus: Let the right way (the way of Jesus) be fixed in your heart. Let your heart be pure with justice, honesty, virtue, and holiness, and be free from wickedness and the ways that lead there.

Your husband: Behave in a moral and just way toward your husband.

Applied

Bride: Yield (willingly give up possession of yourself, your life, and your way) to Jesus and let Him work His way in you. You cannot get there on your own, it takes surrendering (stop resisting and submit to His authority, give yourself back to Him, as it was before He sent you to your mother's womb, that you may fulfill His purpose). You yield and surrender by choosing Jesus and His way. You choose Jesus and His way by vowing to serve Him only and by vowing not to deliberately do, feel, think, nor speak anything against Jesus and His way no matter the cost; and should you go against Him out of ignorance and come to knowledge of the wrong, you will not persist in it but repent, turn, and do right; you must keep and be faithful to Him in this promise. When you choose Him, He will plant and nurture the right way (His way) in you: to be honest and true, to be fair, to be moral, to recognize and reject evil and wickedness. It won't be easy at times, but because you have surrendered to Him you will find it unnatural to be any other way or to do any other thing deliberately, and if you try you *will* feel the struggle within yourself, because you have been changed. Accept that change, do right, and be at peace, even in the storm. If you stumble, stop and quickly turn back to Jesus in true repentance, and your righteousness will be restored; now walk in it being awake.

Wife: Yield to your husband as is suitable in God; behave in a fair, reasonable, moral, honest, and true way toward him. Do not fight against nor act against your husband; if you do, you are fighting and acting against God because God placed him over you. Listen to him and respect the things he says

Live

and asks; do not deliberately say nor do anything you know will displease him. Consider him and be agreed in all decisions.

Love

Jesus: Love Jesus with all of yourself and from the deepest part of yourself. Possess and give the love of God. Love Jesus, love yourself, love others, love those being used as your enemies. Be devoted to, delighted in, and have interest in Jesus and all concerning Him.

Your husband: Love your husband beyond measure, and let it show in the things you say and do.

Applied

Love unconditionally, without expectation of anything in return; without limitations and conditions. If Jesus and your husband and all others don't do what you want when you want, and if you never get your way, you still *must* love them with all your heart and not withhold anything nor any part of you from them. Again, it takes yielding and surrendering to Jesus to receive this kind of love and this strength of love out of Heaven. Jesus will plant and nurture this love (true love) in you, if you are willing. It is a patient love, an enduring love, a forgiving love, a meek love, an understanding love, a love with wisdom, a discerning love, a devoted love, a deep love, a faithful love, a moral love, a love free of evil and wickedness, a love anchored in God, and an eternal love. Don't keep this love locked inside to yourself; express it, not only show your love but tell it also. Tell Jesus you love Him. Tell your husband you love him. Tell all others you love that you love them. Let your love be *felt* and *heard*; never let one abandon the other.

Discretion

(Will preserve you in the way of Jesus.)

Jesus: Discern and separate yourself from all evil and contrary ways, things, thoughts, and deeds.

Your husband: Discern what is in the best interest of the intimacy between you and your husband and the life of your marriage, then act and speak

Restoration

accordingly.

APPLIED

Bride: Do not fight against God; behave with meekness. Listen to and obey Jesus. Speak and act only with His authority; though the truth be within you, it is not always given for you to speak nor act; don't let your good be evil spoken of.

Wife: Do not fight against God through your husband; do not fight against God within you; do not strangle the life from your marriage. Learn about and know your husband. Stop all your stubborn ways; be agreed with your husband as God leads. If your husband makes a mistake, maintain respect toward him.

Truth

Jesus: Be a person of truth; let it lead and guide you.
Your husband: Be genuine toward your husband at all times.

APPLIED

Bride: Speak truth always; do not pollute it at any time for any reason. A faithful servant will not lie. It is OK to joke and have fun, but God will judge all that comes from a wicked heart and deceptions. Be genuine, real, steadfast, loyal, upright, and faithful. Let truth be fixed in you. Truth may cut like a knife and pierce like a sword at times, but when spoken with the love of Jesus it is always best and will serve that person and you well. Truth spoken in love, with mercy and not with an evil heart, is what Jesus desires from all His children. Speak truth or keep silent; let God give you what to say so you will build up and strengthen, not tear down, devour, or destroy that which is good. Also, attend to Jesus so that you will know when to keep quiet (though the truth be in you), and you ought to obey Him.

Wife: Never lie to your husband. Communicate openly with him; he is by your side for you to confide in and share with. Reveal all of who you are and give him all of you. Be genuine, real, steadfast, loyal, and faithful. Know and trust that God has given you to a man who loves you unconditionally as He does.

Live

Strength

Jesus: Jesus is your Rock. He is your Source of mental, emotional, and physical comfort and support. There is no burden too great for Him to share or carry; depend on Him with full trust; He is your all in all.

Your husband: Depend on your husband with full trust, knowing that Jesus is the head of him and has placed you by his side that you may lean on him and rely on him.

Applied

Bride: You must be open (yielded, surrendered) so that God can freely work in you and pour into you that which will wash away double-mindedness, doubt, being afraid, and all in you that is hesitant or against His plan for the results He desires in any situation or purpose. Let Jesus build upon the core of who you are. He has given you authority and power to be in *full* control of your flesh and in *full* control over your enemy, if you so choose. Jesus is also your physical support. He is sufficient where your body lacks, if you have full trust in Him. You have full trust in Him by *knowing* He is able of *all* things; know that nothing is impossible for Him. Not just a saying that you believe it is possible or may be possible, but knowing that there are *no* limitations great nor small in this life or beyond to Jesus. If you ask it and it is in His will and plan for your life or if He said it, never doubt, it will be done; yes, even in your life, but you must know it and trust Him. Some things will be difficult, but rely always on Jesus. Whatever feeling or thought rises up in you against His Word and His plan, rebuke it, and cast it down by giving it to Him and asking Him to wash and cleanse it away. The Father is your storehouse and is faithful to supply all you need for victory in His perfectly appointed time. Have faith knowing the all-mighty and all-powerful God you serve. Have full trust in Jesus; He is strength.

Wife: Be completely open with your husband; lean and rely on him. Jesus will supply him to comfort and support you, and will supply him with all you need in your marriage. Allow your husband to lean on you and rely on you. Jesus will supply you to support and comfort him, and will supply you with all he needs in your marriage. The union of Jesus, your husband, and you form the

Restoration

perfect oneness: complete, whole, in harmony, and an unbreakable bond. There should be and will be nothing missing—no need unmet; Jesus must be present.

Thanks

Jesus: Be thankful to Jesus; He is your God, Savior, and Shepherd. Jesus doesn't have to do anything for you but because He loves you He does.

Your husband: Be thankful to your husband in all he does for you. Out of the love he has for you he does all for you the best he knows how.

Applied

Bride: Show and speak gratitude to Jesus; do not take Him for granted, nor disregard the work of His hands or anything He does for you. His heart desires to be appreciated too. His heart is also weary and grieved by greedy, ungrateful, inconsiderate, and thoughtless children as your heart would be and even more so. Attend to Him not only when you are in need but also continue always after He has been merciful in meeting your need. Appreciate Him just because He is God.

Wife: Show and speak gratitude to your husband. Do not ignore, nor dismiss, nor belittle anything he does for you or for the household; it may not be your way, nor the way of any other husband, nor the best way, but is the way he shows his love. If it is a wrong way, allow God to change him and teach him how to love you. Do not take him for granted. Don't pay attention to him only when you want something from him; he is not by your side to be used nor abused nor taken advantage of. Attend to him always and with love. Appreciate him just because he is your husband, and such is pleasing to God.

Praise

Jesus: Express respect, gratitude, and adoration toward Jesus; glory in Him.

Your husband: Let your husband feel and know that you adore him.

Applied

Bride: Show (by living right and obeying) and tell Jesus how you feel about Him in your inmost being.

Live

Wife: Show (in the way you behave toward him and care for him) and tell your husband how you feel about him in your inmost being.

Trust

Jesus: Accept and believe that Jesus is real and is able to care for you entirely; He's not some far off God but close and personal to you.

Your husband: Accept and believe in your husband to care for you and lead the household.

Applied

Bride: Give Jesus full trust. Allow Him to strip away all you are not and reveal the core of you, the truth of you. Give yourself to Him and know that He will receive you, make you perfect before Him, and be a husband to you. Fear not; He will attend to all your needs in His perfect time.

Wife: Give your husband full trust. Be real with him; be open with him that he may attend to all your needs.

Your Refuge

Jesus: Run to Jesus and abide in Him always, let Him make you a child of Light. He is your hiding place from all that would devour you; He protects and secures you.

Your husband: Run to your husband and not another; he is there to protect you and comfort you. Forget not that you are his refuge also; protect, comfort, and strengthen him in his times of need that he may run always to you and not another.

Applied

Bride: Tell all your troubles to Jesus, go to Him in prayer and read His Word, and He will give you peace or more peace through all that comes against you.

Wife: Share all that bothers you with your husband that he may attend to you in whatever ways he can and to seek God with you for what he is not able. Let your husband share also with you; attend to him in what you are able, and

Restoration

seek God with him for what you are not. If your husband is your cause for distress, then give it to Jesus. He is able.

Your Fortress

Jesus: Your path of light in Jesus is a place fortified against the enemy so that you will not be affected; do not leave this path!

Your husband: A marriage with Jesus as the foundation, center, and head is fortified against the enemy. Make your marriage relationship fortified against its enemies.

Applied

Bride: Have daily communion (sharing and communication) with Jesus in prayer and by talking to Him and reading His Word. He will let you know how to walk in the Light and give you forewarning of the pits and snares ahead that you may avoid them, or to strengthen and encourage you if the pits and snares are those you must pass through in order to build you. He is so merciful in sharing His secrets with you. He delights in your success; He wants you to walk perfect before Him, so He helps, by shining some light into the darkness of your future that you may not stumble and that you may have hope.

Wife: Have daily sharing and communication with your husband and keep God at the head of your relationship. Make Jesus the foundation, center, and head of your marriage by obeying His laws and counsel concerning marriage and seeking Him with your husband in all decisions to be made. You are not only joined with your husband but joined with Jesus also. Leave Him out of nothing, or you will have much trouble. Don't decide first what you want and will do then try to drag Jesus along with you. Don't make Jesus an afterthought, but seek Him first to see if what you think you want is a wise thing or a thing that is in His plan for your life. Whatever you want may not be wrong in general but wrong for you, so seek Him first that you may walk in the path prepared for you—your fortified path. Do not resist your husband and his counsel; trust that the counsel of Jesus is in him to lead you and the household. You are now one, your path is now connected as one.

Live

Your Rock

Jesus: Jesus is the only unmovable One. He is in full control. Nothing moves, shakes, nor disturbs Him. He is unchangeable from the way of truth and light. He is Truth and Light.

Your husband: When your husband stands in Jesus and Jesus is in him, God supplies him to be a constant, unmovable source of strength for you, and you for him.

APPLIED

Bride: Jesus is there for all His children; depend and rely on Him. He is your foundation, your strength, your stability, your anchor. Pray, read His Word consistently, and believe Him; He will get you through the most difficult and impossible-seeming things, and when it's all done it will seem like you have awakened from a dark dream, but you will know Him better and can glory in Him.

Wife: Your husband was given for you to depend on and rely on; lean on him emotionally and physically when needed; he is your support and you are his.

Your Friend

Jesus: Jesus is your close, personal, best friend with absolute counsel. If you choose Him too, you will have a bond of mutual affection with Him like no other. He is your help and support; you can depend on and rely on Him at all times. He will never betray you; see to it that you never betray Him.

Your husband: Your husband should be your best earthly friend; there should be nothing in you or about you that's hid from him. You should confide in each other. Things you can't tell anyone but Jesus should also be shared with your husband, and with God at the head of your marriage, you can trust that nothing revealed will be used against you. A husband that is obedient to Jesus is a husband you can depend on and rely on and reveal your innermost being to without shame nor hesitancy. When true friendship is achieved, you will have a bond of mutual affection with him beyond what you could have ever dreamed.

Restoration

Applied

Bride: Be a friend to Jesus; be faithful and true by thinking of Him and considering Him in your actions and the things you hold to. Do not do any deliberate thing against Him; live in a manner that will cause Him to trust you, not for show but sincerely. Trust and believe Him; possess righteousness and be obedient so that He can rely on you and have trust in you.

Wife: Be a friend to your husband, be a faithful and true friend; keep his secrets and support him unconditionally. Do not do nor speak any deliberate thing against him. Teach him to trust you and to depend and rely on you; teach him that you are his best friend and that he can share the innermost part of himself with you and that you will not betray him. You teach him all this by being consistently good to him with all sincerity.

The Lord Is:

- **Your Habitation**

Jesus: Jesus is your Master and Ruler, the One who created and manages all life and sees to your every need; He is your dwelling place. Let your feet be fixed (permanent) in the path of Light.

Applied

Who or what occupies your thoughts and time? Do you consider Jesus throughout your daily routine? Do you remember Him when things are well with you? Spend time in His presence. Spend time in His Word. Spend time in prayer. Spend time talking to Him. Consider Him and seek Him in planning your day.

- **Your God**

Jesus: Jesus is your Creator and Supreme Ruler. Jesus is the ***only*** God, Creator, Ruler, Savior, and Keeper of the world and ***all*** life; without Him was ***nothing*** made nor can be maintained. He holds all life and all breath in His hand and desires to be near and dear to all He made in His image. God the Father/Jesus: He ever was, He created you, cares for you, authorizes and sees to

Live

all your needs. God the Son/Christ/Jesus: He was from the beginning; He came from the Father, taught and lived the example, suffered, died, rose, ascended back to Heaven, and lives—all for you, that you may be cleansed and saved. God the Holy Ghost/Jesus: He also was from the beginning; He came from the Father by the Son, and is present with you, daily, to perform all God's Word unto you and in you.

Applied

He has given Himself to you; yield and surrender to Him and receive Him.

- **Your Shepherd**

Jesus: Jesus loves you beyond measure. He is your Master and Keeper. It is His pleasure to tend to you and to see that all is well with you. Are you His sheep? Do you look to Him at all times? Do you trust Him at all times? Are you easily led by Him, or are you easily led astray? Are you obedient to His voice?

Applied

Jesus is your guide through this world; don't walk through this life alone, you don't know the true way to victory. Yield to Him and let Him lead you, He knows the very best way. Nothing is hid from Him, He knows where all the thorns, nets, and pits lie. He will lead you into and give you possession of more than you could ever want for yourself, and you will have joy and peace in it. He will tend to you, and you will be whole with a full life. He walked through this life you are living and remained righteous. He knows righteousness is possible in all persons and expects it. He dislikes persistent disobedience. There are things He will not tolerate, and He will correct you as He sees fit; He may even need to break you that you may learn to obey, but there is ***nothing*** He doesn't understand. Never try to hide from Him; give Him ***all*** of you, and He will do in you what is necessary that you may be righteous. His guidance is not only spiritual to guide you into eternity with Him, though that is His ultimate determined goal. His guidance is also earthly guidance through this physical life so that you will live a full life, possessing all He is pleased for you to have and not being affected by any evil, that He may be glorified in you, and He will keep you to that end.

Restoration

- **Your Buckler/Shield**
  (If you walk uprightly.)

  Jesus: Jesus is your keeper, defender, and defensive armor in this war against the enemy. Satan is against Jesus, and, because you belong to Jesus, Satan is also against you. It's never just about you; whatever comes against you, it is not your fight, and by yourself you cannot win. This is why you should give it all to Jesus and not worry, because in Him the victory is already won. *Your enemy* is "the evil one" and his kingdom—because of Truth and Light, *his purpose,* is sin and wrong done by you in serving him—knowing or unknowingly, *his goal* is to swallow you up into darkness—causing your death, as he is dead. *His way* is **fear**—causing distrust in God, also causing all manner of wickedness to alleviate the fear by yourselves, **lust**—of all things that distract from God and are against God, and **carnal pleasure**—pleasure to your flesh, and your pleasure in all things contrary to Jesus. The *tools* and *weapons* he uses are: people/vessels who allow him to; immoral, perverted, and depraved thoughts and ways (all thoughts and ways that conflict with the way of Jesus); feelings (all feelings that conflict with righteousness); things in your daily life; sicknesses, and diseases. In his kingdom, and backing him, are principalities and powers; he is their king; they are his workers of iniquity. Never hate anyone nor anything being used by them; hate evil only, and pray for them (the vessels being used) that they will be delivered to be children of Light, as you were delivered or are about to be. Jesus has already conquered them (the evil one and his workers of iniquity). They have no power against you to affect you unless you choose them by walking in darkness or unless because of you being a child of Light Jesus permits them to affect you to prove and build you in order to take you to another level in Him. In this case, though you may not feel Him, Jesus is with you through it, and if you hold on to Him with full trust it will not destroy you, only refine you.

  ### Applied
  Fully surrender to Jesus. Then by Him, put on the whole armor of God. Let *truth* be secured/fixed in your soul; let *righteousness* reign in your heart. Let your feet be ready and willing, and walk in the path of *peace*; have *faith* (complete trust and confidence/full trust) in Jesus, and nothing will affect/break you. Protect your mind through *salvation* (possess a saved mind,

Live

delivering and preserving it from corruption); possess the *Sword*/the Word (reading consistently with heavenly understanding), so that Jesus may lead and guide you. Don't choose some and cast some away, but believe all His Word; *pray* consistently, in the good and through the bad. Wherever you are and whatever you are doing through the course of each day, maintain constant communication with Jesus (being sincere and humble, being open to Him, and being always ready to seek for a purpose or to be used by Him in a purpose). Never give up on Jesus; He has not given up on you.

Dwell in His Secret Place
Jesus: Live in the heart and will of God by being His child of Light, and walk securely in the path of truth and light which Jesus set you in.
APPLIED
Yield, surrender, submit to Jesus. Walk in the armor of God.

Loving-kindness Every Morning
Jesus: Jesus is merciful and will bring you through all situations into newness.
APPLIED
Ask and trust Him to..., then acknowledge and praise Him.

Faithfulness Every Night
Jesus: Jesus is faithful in times of trouble and at all times.
APPLIED
Give Jesus full trust in every difficulty and evil that comes against you, then acknowledge and praise Him.

Do Not Be a Scorner
Jesus: Do not despise or view neither any person nor thing as worthless or

Restoration

beneath you; all were created by Jesus unto a purpose.
APPLIED
Respect all people and all things, all are the works of the hand of God.

Abstain from wickedness or you will be cursed: As the bride of Jesus Christ, you must avoid all wicked ways, feelings, thoughts, and speech; if you embrace and persist in evil, morally wrong, and trouble-making ways, Jesus will reject you, and sin and its consequences will be allowed to have their way with you. If you stumble or fall, get up and turn quickly back to Jesus in true repentance.

The contrary way is an abomination to your Master and Ruler: Keep from all things and ways that are against Jesus. Rebellious, stubborn, defiant, and presumptuous ways are wicked and evil in His sight; He abhors them. It is not what comes against you, rising up from within you, or from the outside, but what you allow or continuously allow to rest and dwell in you. Cast out and cast off and resist all evil and ways that lead to evil. Let evil find no place of abode nor any room to rest in you.

Don't withhold good from any to whom it is due: Put away selfishness. Do right to others with a ready and willing mind, heart, hands, and feet. Have good thoughts and will toward others. Be like Jesus.

Walk in your path under protection and stumble not:

- *Sound wisdom:* Thorough discernment and good sense will give life to your soul and grace (favor) to your life; let it not leave your way of thinking.
- *Discretion:* Discerning and being discreet will preserve you and give life

Live

to your soul and grace (favor) to your life; let it not leave your way of thinking.

Long Life and Peace

Remember His law: Love. Love your neighbor as yourself; no child of Light hates himself or herself, so as you are good to yourself, in like manner, forgive and be good to **all** others. All the law is fulfilled in love—true love, as God loves. For in that love is no willful wrong nor harm done; in that love is obedience to God and His ways. How does God love? He made you; He is a Father to you. He saved you by pouring out from Himself into the person of Christ, His Son; He is a brother, a friend, your everything. He poured out from Himself into the person of the Holy Ghost; He is your guide, help, strength, leader, counselor, protector, and comforter, and He is there to do all you need, by authority of your Father, and if you are true He is ever with you, though you may not feel Him.

Let your heart keep His commandments: Love. Love Jesus and obey Him. Love yourself by choosing life (right and right things); love all others, as Christ loved you. How did Christ love you? He laid down His life for you. He thought of you first; your welfare came first; so ought you to put Jesus first and to think of others first and meet their needs as God provides you; this is love.

Favor and Good Understanding with God and Man

Mercy: Let not mercy abandon you; make certain you speak with mercy; possess mercy in your heart.

Truth: Let not truth abandon you; make certain you speak with truth; possess truth in your heart.

God's Direction

Have full and complete trust in God: Accept Jesus, accept His Word, have confidence in Him, hope in Him, rely on Him. Is there anyone who knows you better, even better than you know yourself? No, not one, but Jesus only. Just

Restoration

as He knows you, He knows how to care for you better than you know how to care for yourself and better than anyone else can ever care for you.

Lean not to your own understanding: Surrender to Jesus and allow Him to open you so that you will receive His understanding that He may lead you through this life in the path of peace. Not seeking God to know His view and judgment is choosing a destructive path for yourself. Jesus sees the whole picture—you don't; so, unless you are led by Him, how can you possibly not make a mess of things?

Acknowledge God with your whole being: Declare the goodness and mercies of Jesus in everything. He is not ashamed of the work of His hands; He was not ashamed to help you, don't be ashamed to thank Him and make Him known. Don't be ashamed to behave as the child of Light that you are.

Source of Health and Life

Be not wise in your own eyes: You can do nothing effective and lasting in your own power or by your own knowledge; you have no power by yourself; you have no knowledge of yourself. Don't rob God by taking credit for what God has done and what God has placed within you. When others praise you, acknowledge God and take that praise and glory and give it to Jesus and thank Him for using you.

Fear the Lord: Is there anyone or anything that can compare to Jesus? No, not one. Regard your Creator, Master, and Ruler with reverence and awe. There is no like power. There is no like love. There is no like provider. There is none like Him, and He has offered Himself to you; respect Him, love Him, receive Him, acknowledge Him, and live right.

Depart from evil: Separate yourself from evil, turn out of the way of evil, and avoid every evil in all its forms. Compromise not toward any evil. Do not cast away any offender nor those yet to be drawn into the Light—you must love them—only reject the acceptance of all their wrong within you for your own way. You must not conform to darkness, but let the darkness be conformed to the Light, being transformed by the hand of God and the Light shining from within you. What is evil? Evil is **all** things and ways that are against (contrary

Live

to) God. God is Righteousness (the **right** way), let righteousness reign (prevail and rule) in you. All things, great or small, that are contrary to the **right** way is evil and should be resisted.

*Despise not the chastening of your Shepherd, Master, and Ruler; neither be weary of His correction, because He loves you and delights in you, so He corrects you. He wants you to be the very best **you** that He desired when He thought of you and sculpted you in the womb.*

Find **Wisdom** and get **Understanding**: To obtain it is better than obtaining silver, and to increase in it is better than to increase in fine gold. It is more precious than rubies, and all the things you can ever desire cannot be compared to it, for it is too excellent. Full extent of time is on one side of it, and riches and honor on the other side of it. Use it in all things, and your method and manner of doing all things will be a method and manner that is pleasant and in the direction of peace. It is a source of life to you if it be established in you and used by you, and you will have joy if you keep it. By wisdom God founded the earth; by understanding He established the heavens; by His knowledge the depths (the deepest, lowest, inmost parts) are broken up, and the clouds drop down dew.

Section II

Stand

Remember, O Lord, what is come upon us: consider, and behold our reproach. Our inheritance is turned to strangers, our houses to aliens. We are orphans and fatherless, our mothers are widows. We have drunken our water for money; our wood is sold unto us. Our necks are under persecution: we labour, and have no rest. We have given the hand to the Egyptians, and to the Assyrians, to be satisfied with bread. Our fathers have sinned, and are not; and we have borne their iniquities. Servants have ruled over us: there is none that doth deliver us out of their hand. We gat our bread with the peril of our lives because of the sword of the wilderness. Our skin was black like an oven because of the terrible famine. They ravished the women in Zion, and the maids in the cities of Judah. Princes are hanged up by their hand: the faces of the elders were not honoured. They took the young men to grind, and the children fell under the wood. The elders have ceased from the gate, the young men from their musick. The joy of our heart is ceased; our dance is turned into mourning. The crown is fallen from our head: woe unto us, that we have sinned! For this our heart is faint; for these things our eyes are dim. Because of the mountain of Zion, which is desolate, the foxes walk upon it. Thou, O Lord, remainest for ever; Thy throne from generation to generation. Wherefore dost Thou forget us for ever, and forsake us so long time? Turn Thou us unto Thee, O Lord, and we shall be turned; renew our days as of old. But Thou hast utterly rejected us; Thou art very wroth against us.

Blessed is the man that trusteth in the Lord, and whose hope the Lord is. For he shall be as a tree planted by the waters, and that spreadeth out her roots

Restoration

by the river, and shall not see when heat cometh, but her leaf shall be green; and shall not be careful in the year of drought, neither shall cease from yielding fruit. The heart is deceitful above all things, and desperately wicked: who can know it? I the Lord search the heart, I try the reins, even to give every man according to his ways, and according to the fruit of his doings. As the partridge sitteth on eggs, and hatcheth them not; so he that getteth riches, and not by right, shall leave them in the midst of his days, and at his end shall be a fool. A glorious high throne from the beginning is the place of our sanctuary.

Possess and Abound In:

Diligence
Bride: *Be thorough in performing your duties as the bride of Christ.*
Wife: Be thorough in performing your wifely duties to your husband.

Faith
Bride: *Hear the Word of the Lord, My chosen, and My people. Thus saith the Lord of hosts, the God of Israel; Behold, I will bring evil upon this place, the which whosoever heareth, his ears shall tingle. Thus saith the Lord of hosts; Even so will I break this people and this city, as one breaketh a potter's vessel, that cannot be made whole again.*
Wife: Have complete trust (acceptance of the truth of a statement without evidence of investigation) and confidence (belief and assurance that you can rely on the abilities) in your husband. He is given under the authority of God for you to rely on (depend on with full trust) and confide (have full trust) in.

Virtue
Bride: *Possess moral excellence and perfection, be pure and faithful to Jesus.*
Wife: Have moral perfection, be pure and faithful in your vows and the

Stand

laws of marriage till you are called **_home_**.

Knowledge
Bride: *O My people, return to the Lord your God; for you have fallen by your iniquity. Take with you words, and turn to the Lord: say unto Him, Take away all iniquity, and receive us graciously: so will we render the offerings of our lips. Priests and deacons, ministers shall not save us: we will not depend upon our minds: neither will we say anymore to the work of our hands, you are our gods: for in Thee the fatherless findeth mercy.*

Wife: Know yourself—who Jesus has made you. Know your husband—who Jesus has made him. Know all you have been fore-taught by Jesus. Remember and know all you will be taught in the process of your relationship. Receive, possess, and perform the good you have been and will be taught. Release and cast away the bad you experience—never forgetting its consequences, that you will from then on avoid every such pit without affect to you, your husband, your relationship/marriage, your family, or your household.

Temperance
Bride: *Fear God and give reverence to Him, He is merciful and faithful to all His children. Who is strong like the Lord? Who is faithful like the Lord? The heavens are His, He has founded the world and the fullness thereof, all are His creation, we shall rejoice in Him. The Lord is your strength, your defense, and your King.*

Wife: Have full self-control. Be strong in the Lord. Though there be no fault found in you, hold your peace when it is not given (appropriate) for you to speak. Forgive the act against you, trust God to see you through.

Patience
Bride: *Wait on the Lord and trust Him. What He has promised, that will He do in a time that is right and just for you.*

Wife: Wait on God....

Restoration

GODLINESS
Bride: *Remain awake and live in righteousness, that you may be ready at His coming.*

Wife: Be devoted to your husband, be deeply and earnestly sincere to him and in all things concerning him.

KINDNESS
Bride: *Possess and perform kindness to all.*

Wife: Be kind, considerate, generous, affectionate, loving, gentle, and well meaning to your husband. Do him no harm. Cause him no deliberate trouble nor difficulty. Give willingly and freely to him. Show him without hesitation how you feel about him—that you like and enjoy him. Show him great care and love. Accept everything about him, even his faults, imperfections, and weaknesses. Be well-mannered and respectful toward him always. Give attention to him and acknowledge him as the gift he is: your husband, and God's child. Let your thoughts, words, behavior, and actions, which are expressed and done to him and toward him, come out of the love Jesus has planted and raised and anchored in you. Be natural and have fun with him.

CHARITY
Bride: *Love everyone and everything as Jesus loves.*

Wife: Love your husband fully and completely with the love Jesus has planted and nurtured and anchored in you; a love pure and clean and genuine and free from deceit, a love deeply anchored in Jesus. Give your husband all of you, and in return receive all of him, and be both one in Jesus.

Also:

Stand

Mercy
Bride: Possess compassion and forgiveness and perform them—as Jesus has likewise been merciful to you.
Wife: Be compassionate and forgiving if your husband does something to offend you—as you were often forgiven your ***many*** offenses against him without complaint; ease his distress or pain always.

Meekness
Bride: Submit to Jesus and His way.
Wife: Be soft and gentle and welcoming toward your husband.

Prudence
Bride: Attend to Jesus and your Christian life that your relationship with Him die not. Intimacy with Jesus is vital. Let Jesus in to the innermost part of you, even to the soul.
Wife: Show care and thought to the life of your marriage that it die not. Intimacy of the heart, mind, and body with your husband is vital; let him in to the innermost part of you.

Longsuffering
Bride: Lean on Jesus, He is a husband to you, also your nearest and dearest friend. ***He is your strength*** *(when you put "full trust" in Him)* ***through all*** *(notice the words "through" and "all")* ***problems, challenges, provocation, tests, and "all" seasons that come against you.*** *Provoke Him not in any moment of weakness, but ask of Him and He will give you more strength to endure. He loves you so.*
Wife: Lean on your husband as you both lean on Jesus. Let Jesus be your strength, and be patient through all problems and challenges and all provocation. Provoke not your husband, and, should he provoke you, forgive him. Let not ***any*** thing, without (coming from the outside) nor within (coming from within you), gain access to affect you or harm your marriage—

Restoration

interrupting or preventing intimacy of your heart, mind, and body with your husband. Jesus is your strength; wisdom, knowledge, understanding, and truth are with Him; trust Him.

FORBEARING

Bride: *Always know and attend to who you are (the bride of Christ) and behave in like manner; He will attend to all your needs and situations.*

Wife: Have patience and self-control always. Attend always to your vows and wifely duties. You are the wife given to your husband, behave in like manner always. It is too late to change your mind; you are already one; you were made/molded to fit him, you **must** live as one flesh. Give all that rises up in you or comes against you to Jesus and trust Him; He will attend to it.

FORGIVENESS

Bride: *Forgive and release much, as you have been forgiven much and as Jesus has released all you have done to the depths of the sea. Also, knowing that you may yet still desire much forgiveness along this path of love and peace, it is vital that you willingly and readily forgive and release, always.*

Wife: Do not have nor indulge in anger nor hate; willingly and readily forgive and release your husband's offenses, mistakes, wrongdoings, inappropriateness, and flaws; do not hold any resentment toward him nor toward anything in or about your marriage. Admit to yourself and accept his imperfections, faults, weaknesses, and brokenness, and cover him. Pray and desire good for him (what Jesus has placed in you to be prayed), and release him with your prayer into the hand of Jesus. Then put "full trust" in Jesus for what you have prayed while being the wife to him that Jesus called you to be, and fear (reverence and stand in awe of) God as He (**not you**) molds your husband to fit you as the husband He desires and called him to be. Though some things and habits may take time to be broken and loosed from him and your marriage, keep full trust in Jesus and keep being a godly wife; the change will manifest. You will first notice the change in yourself (as you yourself also need to be

Stand

changed)—this is the encouragement and hope Jesus has placed in you, that your prayer has touched Him, that He is attending to you and your situation. Acknowledge and thank Jesus in the minute (**extremely** small) changes as well as the great changes; also, acknowledge and appreciate your husband in these changes.

THANKFULNESS
Bride: *Show gratitude to Jesus in all He does. Be thankful to everyone; to dismiss them and their deeds is to dismiss Jesus, so show gratitude toward others. See Him, feel Him, and acknowledge Jesus daily, and, moment by moment, He is always active and attending to you. Stop! Breathe! That is Jesus; thank Him; and, He does so much more for you, seen and unseen. He loves you so.*

Wife: Reassure your husband that you are pleased with him. Understand, acknowledge, and show gratitude toward him in all his deeds and efforts toward you. Never take your husband nor your marriage for granted; your marriage is a blessed union and gift from God; he is the husband given to you/molded by God to fit you; he is the other side of you. Appreciate him always.

HUMBLENESS OF MIND
Bride: *Jesus is first above all things and persons; make Him so with you. Be modest in all manner and behavior, acknowledging Jesus always.*

Wife: After Jesus, think of your husband; put him before all things and persons earthly. Make him and the life of your marriage a priority above ***all*** else. Be modest in all manner and behavior as a godly wife, acknowledging Jesus and holding great respect for your husband and marriage, that other women and wives not yet in the Light of true intimacy may know the way.

HEART RULED BY PEACE
Bride: *Have peace by abiding in Jesus and letting His way/manner be manifested in you and performed by you always.*

Restoration

Wife: Abide in Jesus so that you will have and exhibit control over your emotions, and so your heart will remain free from anxiety and distress, so that nothing will stretch apart and choke your marriage.

Overcome and Put Off and Abstain From:

Fornication

Bride: Avoid all things and ways that rob Jesus of being first in your life and cause you to turn out of the way of God.

Wife: Avoid untoward behaviors and sexual behaviors:

Avoid all forms of immoral (self-indulgent) behaviors and sexual behaviors in your marriage; make certain your marriage and marital bed remains always undefiled (uncorrupted, undestroyed, unspoiled, free of wickedness and guiltiness, healthy, and whole). Never allow another person to touch you in an improper way; you belong to your husband. Flirting is an inviting act and way: Never flirt with anyone but your husband only. Avoid unruly behavior (being difficult) with your husband and in your marriage. Avoid lack of inclination toward your husband and your marriage. Avoid deliberate annoying behaviors with your husband in your marriage. Avoid being froward (willfully contrary) with your husband and in your marriage. Avoid perverse (willful, persistent, obstinate) determinations against your husband and marriage. Avoid improper social behaviors against your husband and your marriage. Avoid all that is unfavorable with your marriage and vows.

Uncleanness

Bride: Remain pure in spirit; avoid all that would pollute your Christianity. Do not be deliberate nor stubborn against God or He cannot use you and will turn His face away so that He doesn't have to look on your filthiness.

Wife: Avoid all filthy (foul, vulgar, vile, contemptible, offensive) and immoral (violating) ways and acts that would pollute and dishonor your marriage and vows. Do not entertain, encourage, practice, nor entice your

Stand

husband into ways and acts that would pollute intimacy God's way and dishonor your husband and marriage. Do not adapt the vile, violating ways and deeds of the world into your marriage. Remember God is the head; adapt His ways and deeds. Remain chaste (pure in thought and deed) toward each other and with your marriage.

INORDINATE AFFECTION

Bride: *Love Jesus most. Do not allow your affection and love for Jesus to be polluted; everything about God has order, though you may not see.*

Wife: Avoid all unacceptable and wrong tastes and appetites; avoid likes and desires not in order nor in line with God and which are against your husband and a godly marriage.

EVIL CONCUPISCENCE

Bride: *Yearn after Jesus only, not after people and things and ways that will profit you nothing but darkness and death. Avoid all that would pollute and destroy your intimacy with Jesus.*

Wife: Avoid all lusts, longings, and yearnings after things profoundly immoral, harmful, depraved, and wicked that are against your husband and your marriage. Avoid all ways, things, and people that work consistently and deliberately against your husband and your marriage to pollute and destroy it. Avoid all that would pollute and destroy your intimacy with your husband and the intimacy in your marriage.

COVETOUSNESS/IDOLATRY

Bride: *Jesus is the only God; besides (other than/in addition to) Him there is none, and none can compare. All other persons and things are false, a lie, and a deception. There is no luck nor fortune, there is only Jesus and His will and allowance for all things and all people and the opportunities He gives and allows. Worship Jesus only. Let your deepest desire be toward Him only, and He will direct*

Restoration

you in all His ways and in all things appropriate.

Wife: Never yearn after, hold excessive admiration for, nor be desirous of any person or thing that does not belong to you. Let your desire be to your husband and all that is yours as is fit (suitable) in God.

ANGER

Bride: *Avoid anger. Anger and wrath belong to God; He alone has the right to be angry and wrathful because of our wickedness and our destruction of the work of His hand, both within us and around us.*

Wife: Avoid or control all feelings in you that would lead to anger; give to God all feelings and thoughts that don't belong in you.

WRATH

Bride: *Jesus cannot use a person with no self-control. If wrath dwells in or is often welcomed in you, you are of no good use to Jesus. Let God fix it.*

Wife: Avoid wrath (extreme anger) completely. This emotion does not belong to you and cannot be handled by you; it will only serve to destroy you and those around you, including your intimacy with your husband; also, the relationship with your children and all others. Let God fix it.

MALICE

Bride: *To be and remain a child of Light,* **ready forgiveness** *is necessary—you must possess it; it must be fixed in you. Never harbor evil, it will kill your intimacy with Jesus.*

Wife: Never harbor nor possess ill will, ill feelings, nor ill thoughts against your husband nor household, neither resent your marriage—it will kill everything you truly want and need.

Stand

BLASPHEMY
*Bride: Possess and keep the fear (reverence and awe) of God. Never speak against nor curse neither God nor the work of His hand. Your love and respect for Him and all that is holy should never be dependent on your circumstance nor your gain. When you are in a wilderness, love and respect Him. When you have loss, love and respect Him. When things don't go your way or seem to be against you, love and respect Him. Whatever your situation, love and respect Him. You don't see the whole picture as He does; don't cause yourself to lose the good His heart desires for you and all He would perform for you. If you were brought forth to experience an entire life of **hard testimony** for His purpose, love and respect Him—even as you draw your last breath. When you love and respect and obey Him in any and all situations, you are precious to Him; He will treasure you, and peace will be made to abide in you.*

Wife: Never do nor speak any evil wicked thing that mocks or disrespects or insults or is against God and the sacred bond of your marriage.

FILTHY COMMUNICATION
Bride: As a child of Light you ought to avoid all filthy and offensive communication. Be careful what you say not only with your lips but also with your body and your behavior. The world is watching; do not cause Jesus and all Heaven shame nor make a mockery of them.

Wife: Avoid all filthy and offensive communication outside your marriage and also within your marriage. Your body and behaviors speak much, also, guard your tongue and lips. Do not cause your husband and your household shame nor make a mockery of them. With all sincerity—be an excellent wife to your husband and an excellent role model for other wives.

LIES
Bride: You must speak truth always. Jesus has no use for a liar. He is truth, and if you lie you have no part in Him.

Wife: Never lie to your husband, nor mislead him, nor practice deceit with him.

Restoration

EVIL
Bride: *Evil has no place in a child of Light. If you possess evil, or it entices you, you must surrender to Jesus and be cleansed.*

Wife: Resist and avoid all forms of evil in your marriage. If you harbor evil or act against your husband, you are also acting against yourself and against God, because you are all joined in the marriage as one. Turn to Jesus and let Him find and pluck out the root of the evil and restore you, as you ought to be.

GUILE
Bride: *Be a child of Light and be sincere in all your ways and toward all people. The deceitful way is contrary to God. Use not deceit nor trickery to attain what you need; Jesus is enough, and all your needs will be met if you trust Him.*

Wife: Avoid all cunning intelligence and deceitful ways and characteristics—they are an enemy to your intimacy with your husband and Jesus. Communicate your needs appropriately (at a time and in a way that does not degrade, disrespect, nor belittle him). Communicate plainly and sincerely to your husband, and to Jesus also; then, trust Jesus and trust your husband that all your needs will be met. Be patient and forgiving while Jesus works it out.

Always maintain the integrity and health of the relationship and marriage. There are ***only*** two in the relationship and marriage with God—which are you and God, ***no more***. There are ***only*** three in the relationship and marriage with your husband—which are you, your husband, and God, ***no more***.

Section III

Virtue

Therefore now amend your ways and your doings, and obey the voice of the Lord your God; and the Lord will repent Him of the evil that He hath pronounced against you. As for me, behold, I am in your hand: do with me as seemeth good and meet unto you. But know ye for certain, that if ye put me to death, ye shall surely bring innocent blood upon yourselves, and upon this city, and upon the inhabitants thereof: for of a truth the Lord hath sent me unto you to speak all these words in your ears.

Hear, ye children, the instruction of a father, and attend to know understanding. For I give you good doctrine, forsake ye not my law. For I was my father's son, tender and only beloved in the sight of my mother. He taught me also, and said unto me, Let thine heart retain my words: keep my commandments and live.

Get wisdom, get understanding: forget it not; neither decline from the words of my mouth. Forsake her not, and she shall preserve thee: love her, and she shall keep thee. Wisdom is the principal thing; therefore get wisdom: and with all thy getting get understanding. Exalt her, and she shall promote thee: she shall bring thee to honour, when thou dost embrace her. She shall give to thine head an ornament of grace: a crown of glory shall she deliver to thee. Hear, O my son, and receive my sayings; and the years of thy life shall be many. I have taught thee in the way of wisdom; I have led thee in right paths. When thou goest, thy steps shall not be straitened; and when thou runnest, thou shalt not stumble. Take fast hold of instruction; let her not go: keep her; for she is thy life. Enter not into the path of the wicked, and go not in the way

Restoration

of evil men. Avoid it, pass not by it, turn from it, and pass away. For they sleep not, except they have done mischief; and their sleep is taken away, unless they cause some to fall. For they eat the bread of wickedness, and drink the wine of violence. But the path of the just is as the shining light, that shineth more and more unto the perfect day. The way of the wicked is as darkness: they know not at what they stumble. My son, attend to my words; incline thine ear unto my sayings. Let them not depart from thine eyes; keep them in the midst of thine heart. For they are life unto those that find them, and health to all their flesh. Keep thy heart with all diligence; for out of it are the issues of life. Put away from thee a froward mouth, and perverse lips put far from thee. Let thine eyes look right on, and let thine eyelids look straight before thee. Ponder the path of thy feet, and let all thy ways be established. Turn not to the right hand nor to the left: remove thy foot from evil.

Be of Inner Beauty

- **A meek and quiet spirit:**
  Be selfless and maintain self-control. Be like Christ.
  Consider your husband first, and maintain self-control with him.
- **Possess a good heart and do good:**
  Possess and perform righteousness, remember the laws, statutes, and judgments given by God, and obey them.
  Possess and perform consistently toward your husband according to the laws, statutes, judgments, and commandments given by God.
- **Be of one mind:**
  Be one with Jesus that you may know what is the right way and walk in it, and that you may live and be fruitful.
  When you are of one mind and in agreement with your husband and put full trust in him, anything you both aim at will be on target and perfectly accomplished. Be of one accord in heart and mind with him and work together with him consistently; you are an help **meet** for him (an help **made to fit** him).

Virtue

- **Subjection:**
*Be subject to God and His ways. He is your Master and Shepherd, depend on Him. Jesus is the supreme authority over you, and whether you acknowledge Him or not He is your all; without Him you are **not**.*
Be subject to your husband. You are under his authority by God. You are to depend on him with full trust. He was given by your side for you to rely on. You were made to affect each other, to be perfectly aligned and in harmony with each other. When he is guided by God, he will come through for you and meet your needs; he will love and care for you perfectly, as you do him.
- **Submit:**
Yield to Jesus; all you need will be found in Him when you surrender.
Submit to your husband as it is fit (suitable, right and appropriate) in God. Accept and yield to the wisdom, knowledge, and understanding God has given him. Discuss everything with him; do not exclude him from any decision. Hide no thing from him. Be on one accord with him. Be agreed (in agreement) with him in all things. Give him your heart, mind, and body, and receive his.
Do not submit to nor accept abuse. Abuse is not suitable, right, nor appropriate in God. You were both made to love and support and serve each other, not to accept abuse from him in any form nor to give abuse to him in any form. If you are suffering or you are an abuser, know that no one is beyond reach of the arm and hand of God. [To the suffering woman: Jesus is able to deliver you and change you from any way or thought or belief that you are deserving of your suffering. You were made to be loved unconditionally, and will receive this love if you allow God to do that complete work in you, that you may know yourself and the treasure that you are. You will love yourself and love as you were meant to love, and love who you were meant to love]. [To the abusive woman (those deliberately so and those who lack control): Jesus is able to deliver you and change you from that wicked way and thought and belief. Yield to Jesus and let Him do that complete work in you. Yield to Jesus and you will gain the control you truly seek to have, which is

Restoration

in truth only control of yourself. Control of yourself (of your emotions) is the only control you need, will ever need, and should have, and Jesus will give that to you. Yield to Jesus and seek earnestly from Him the unconditional love you need, and you will receive it also; and when you find it in you, share it freely and unconditionally as you have received of God. Love Jesus, love yourself, and love your husband with this love. If you are also a stubborn woman or your heart finds pleasure in the misuse of your husband, know that if you persist in your wicked, abusive ways that the same arm and hand of God that is able to reach and heal you to wholeness is also able to reach and expose and punish you, that you may know that He is God, and you ***will*** yield to Him. Don't wait to be punished in order to learn and be changed. Turn from your wicked ways and be the wife that will bring Jesus glory, the wife He is pleased in and has created you to be].

- **Give honor:**

Give honor always to Jesus; it is a great privilege to be a child of God.
Give honor always to your husband. It is a great privilege to be a wife—his wife. Take not your husband nor your marriage for granted; it is a blessed union.

The marriage relationship is a thoughtful, loving, kind, caring, tender, and beautiful gift of God for one human and one help meet that were made to fit each other.

Do not look on and wish after the qualities of other husbands; the husband you have, with all his qualities, is whom it pleased God for you to have. Honor your marriage and honor the man that was made to fit you; though God may not be through with him, don't wait for the finished man, love him unconditionally as he is. If having and giving unconditional love and honor to your husband has been nonexistent or difficult for you, then seek Jesus earnestly for it, and He will plant it deep within you and nourish it. Once you find it in you, let it flow freely to your husband, whether or not you feel he presently deserves it—that is the purpose of this love. He is yours; do not hesitate for fear of the great change that will be seen. To give him that great love

Virtue

is not to be defeated but to win because you will gain the intimacy you both are dying inside for but refused to admit. If he rejects this new, wonderful love, it is because his trust in you has been broken, maybe even for years, or maybe there never was trust. But be consistent toward him in all your ways so he will learn to trust you and know that this new, wonderful love, is real. God knows you both, and the gifts He gives you both are given to be shared between you; so when God gives you this love, it is because He knows that it will be received and reciprocated, though it may take much, much patience on your part. It is a love that you ought not be ashamed of nor hide. Trust Jesus, He never fails.

- **Compassion:**
Be concerned with the welfare of others and help them, as you are able and led by God.
Let your husband feel and know that you are with him and by his side through thick and thin. Let him know, that come what may: you suffer together - you celebrate together; you cry together - you laugh together. Let him know that you are his and you are one. Let him know that he never has to feel insecure about you. Let him know that he never has to hold back nor hide any part of himself [his thoughts or his dreams] from you. Let him know that you support and believe in him, and that you support and believe in the call on his life. Don't separate him from his passion; stand with him and pray for him that all will manifest concerning his passion, as God would have it.

- **Pity:**
Have and show compassion toward others.
Be pitiful toward your husband: being always sympathetic and empathetic toward his stresses and struggles. Let him lean on you, and bear him up as he leans on you; God will be your strength for him. Let him feel and know your devotion to him and that you accept him—all of him.

- **Be courteous:**
Be considerate and respectful to others; let Christ be seen in you.

Restoration

Be always respectful and considerate to your husband. He is a child of God and the one given to you. Take him not for granted but appreciate him and be good to him always. Treat him well, care for him, and love him, as you do yourself. If you love not yourself, then seek Jesus earnestly and He will give you that love for yourself so you can love your husband abundantly and unconditionally and be good to him.

- **Seek peace:**

Children of Light, seek peace as is pleasing to the Lord.
Always search for, find, and practice peace with your husband. Let nothing and no one between; let nothing and no one affect (corrupt), rob, or destroy your intimacy with your husband.

- **Ensue peace:**

Children of Light, follow peace as is pleasing to the Lord.
Always follow (be led by), act in accordance with, and practice peace because of your husband and for the sake of your marriage. The contrary will bring him shame also—for you are one—and may devour the intimacy between you.

- **Bless:**

Praise Jesus always, for He is worthy. Acknowledge Him and all the work of His hand that others may see Him and come to know Him.
Praise your husband consistently, and call on God always on his behalf for favor and protection to him. Let not your praises of him remain within you or be only about him to others but let it be also to him, that he may be encouraged and strengthened as head of your family.

- **Love:**

Love Jesus with all your heart, and with all your soul, and with all your strength, and with all your mind. Love your neighbor as yourself. Go, and be a neighbor (one obedient to God; showing thought, compassion, and care for others).
Possess, maintain, and give your husband fervent love, beyond measure, unconditionally and continually as God gives you.

- **Hospitality:**

Be hospitable to others as is pleasing to God.

Virtue

Show your husband hospitality, being always friendly and generous to him even more so than you do to those you know not.
- **Minister:**
Be a servant of God; let Him use you according to His will.
Serve your husband well out of the ability given to you of God. Attend to his needs and give to him through all means which God has given you to serve him and has made you to help him.
- **Willing:**
Possess and apply willingness toward Jesus always; let Him use you, as He will.
Seek to and work willingly with your hands, feet, heart, and mind. Seek of your husband and know what needs to be done and be in agreement with him, and help, and do your part with all your heart and to the best of your ability. In everything, you both are a team; this is how Jesus sees you. You are not blameless nor free from any responsibility in your marriage or purpose together. Be of relevance in your marriage; apply willingness also toward your husband himself, always.
- **Communicate:**
Communicate with Jesus and with others as a child of Light.
Speak to and communicate with your husband always in a way that is pleasing to God. Share your entire self (all aspects of you - heart, mind, and body) with him, because it is the good way, and also that he will better know how to meet your needs. Be in all ways connected with your husband. Let Jesus bind you and your husband together in Him.
- **Be sober:**
Take thought toward God in earnest, and be not affected by the enemy in all forms that they come.
Be sincere, earnest, thoughtful, and attend to your husband and the life of your marriage.
- **Be vigilant:**
Keep watch concerning your relationship with Jesus; guard it, let nothing and no one between.
Keep careful watch and remain awake concerning your marriage, root out and cast off all that is within you against it and give to Jesus all that

Restoration

comes against it from the outside. Let no thing or person between you and your husband.

- **Be prudent:**

Show thought and care to your intimacy with Jesus by strengthening and maintaining it.

Act with and show thought and care to the purpose and to the life of your marriage.

- **Nurture:**

Nurture your intimacy with Jesus.

Nurture your husband and your intimacy with him. Protect and care lovingly for him. Feed your marriage with nourishment. Seek and know Jesus and His ways and apply them in your relationship.

- **Wickedness:**

Surrender to Jesus and let all wickedness and all ways that lead to wickedness be cleansed from within you.

Speak no wickedness to your husband nor to others about him. Never possess nor communicate anything to him in any manner that makes him feel like less than who he is. Never possess nor communicate anything to anyone in anyway that belittles or degrades him. Never be deliberate against him. Always respect him, honor him, lift him up, and cover him in private and before ***all*** others. Be good to him and pray good for him. Always stand by his side.

- **Speak with no guile in lips:**

Speak not with deception to another, lest you also deceive yourself and fall further into darkness; deception is also a thing abhorred in the presence of God. Let truth and sincerity be fixed in you.

Never possess nor communicate deception and trickery, never behave in any cunning manner toward nor against your husband.

- **Speak not with an evil tongue:**

Speak with wisdom and understanding that you slay not yourself nor another.

Never possess nor communicate poison to your husband, the marriage, the children, nor any of the household: "Be good to them."

Virtue

- **Deny:**
Never deny Jesus and all He is and has done, neither betray Him; acknowledge Him and make Him your all.
Do not deny nor betray your husband. Never be reluctant toward him, nor struggle against him, nor deny him in anything he asks and expects. He loves you, and as a son of God, would not cause you harm. He is your friend, and he is the other side of you, so be free and put full trust in him.
- **Evil:**
Resist all forms of evil; be filled with Light.
Do not render evil for evil toward your husband. Never give nor pay back unpleasant, wicked, immoral, depraved, harmful, undesirable, condescending, insulting, nor degrading thoughts and words and deeds to him. Give it all to Jesus.
- **Rail:**
Never rail against God; surrender to Jesus and have full trust in Him.
Do not render railing for railing toward your husband. If he puts up a wall or barrier, never put up one of your own. If he shuts you out, never do the same. Let him know and see that he can put ***full trust*** in you; you are the other side of him, made and placed by his side for him to rely on. Let him know you are his friend. If he gets loud or shouts at you, never do the same. Give it all to Jesus.
- **Grudge:**
Never murmur nor grumble against God; trust that Jesus knows best.
Have no grudging toward your husband nor in your marriage. Never murmur nor grumble nor give him **"the silent treatment."** Never have nor hold ill intentions and resentment, never be cold toward him, never be ill-tempered nor unwilling toward him nor toward anything he asks or expects of you.

Excel:

Bring substance in your marriage; stand firm in your marriage; bring life into your marriage as God gives.

Restoration

Rise up before the day and pray fervently for strength to your household that Jesus may be in the midst of you all; also for strength and guidance in your tasks ahead.

Examine any problem or battle against the marriage and household and face it; take hold of it, and with the guidance and tools the Lord has given you, overcome it and turn it around and receive good, blessing, growth, and strength from it.

Abide in Jesus and be prepared, strengthened, and armored for what is to come.

Understand that all Jesus has planted and nurtured and raised within you is very good, so be confident; be confident in Jesus having always ***full and complete trust*** in Him; be a confident wife, be a confident mother, be confident in your purpose, be confident in who you are.

Be of strength and light in times of darkness.

Take hold of Jesus in all concerns, to prevent or contain and keep them under control.

Pray and care for the natural and spiritual poor and needy.

Fear not any harsh, bitter times that come against your household, for all are covered and armored with the blood of Christ Jesus, and nothing will affect you.

Abide in Jesus, causing all to be covered by Jesus through His foresight, counsel, and privileges given to you.

Your husband was already established from the beginning when he is set in authority in the midst of the leaders of the nation.

Gain, possess, and maintain a pure, true, and deeply intimate relationship with Jesus, and cause the wayward to turn to Him, the lost to be drawn to Him, the dead to awaken unto Him, the hungry to be fed, the thirsty to be drawn to Him and drink of Him, the naked to be clothed, and provide encouragement and support to the weak and worn because of the life you live and the way Jesus uses you.

Obey Jesus that He may clothe you with strength and honor during hard times, and you shall rejoice in time to come when you have passed through.

Speak with wisdom and a kind tongue habitually.

Virtue

Guide the household with purpose under the authority of Jesus through your husband.

Cause your children and your husband to be of higher standard by being the wife and mother and person Jesus has taught and made you to be, and they will respect and treasure you.

Excel in virtue (possess and perform exceptionally well, in an unusually thorough way in moral integrity).

Showing preferential treatment and an approving attitude to any person, thing, or way that is in error, no matter what or who, is deceitful, intentionally misleading, fraudulent, and a lie. Also, things and ways that look very good, very pleasing, and enticing are empty and without substance: but always attend (listen and pay close attention) to the Lord with reverence (deep respect) and awe (wonder and dread), and you will be respected and admired because of Him.

All you have done and have spoken you will receive and possess, and you will have all reciprocated to you for your obedience to the Lord from the beginning.

The Principles of Marriage:
Bride. Wife.

- *Yield to Jesus.* Submit, surrender, and give back (reciprocate) to your husband good, genuine, devoted, expected, required, and respectful ways; you were made his own, specially, by God. You strictly belong to him; let him have devotedly and unselfishly what he seeks of you whenever he desires without thinking of any profit to yourself.
- *You are the vessel of the Lord; let Him use you as He will. You are not able of yourself; you need Jesus.* Your husband is not able of himself but needs you; neither are you able of yourself but need your husband. You are no longer independent to do as you like, but one flesh, given to each other's care and trust. "Do well unto him."
- *Do not cheat God of yourself nor cheat yourself of all God wants to be to*

Restoration

you; give Him all of you. Maintain intimacy with Jesus that the enemy find no occasion to gain access nor rest in you because of your separation from Him. Do not avoid your husband, cheat him, nor deprive him of yourself (heart, mind, and body). Hold no part of yourself back from him except with mutual consent for a time to fast and pray, and when the time of fasting and prayer is complete, reach for and respond to him vigorously and passionately, uniting again heart, mind, and body that the evil one will have no occasion to gain any access in you against him nor in him against you because of your continuous separation.
- *Never leave Jesus.* Never leave, nor hide, nor run from, nor turn from, nor separate from, nor divorce your husband in any way or form, neither physically nor emotionally; till physical deaths do you part—when Jesus calls you home. Jesus is able.
- *Be always reconciled with Jesus.* Be always reconciled with your husband, be always one with him as you were made. Be both single in the love, the desire, the direction, and the purpose God has called you both to and placed in you both. Husband and wife; exist/live and be truly one in God. "Be ye one flesh."

Postface

How to use this book.
After you have read it through, keep it near, and, daily, after you have communed with God, take one part or a portion of a part, whatever you can handle, and **"live"** it, till it be firm in you. Let these things not remain something you have to try to remember or think hard on, but let it become an extension of yourself, a possession, your nature. Do not resist, but allow God to change and build you, to remove and cast away all in you that does not belong, to work all He has given in this book and even deeper things into you, and so, you will be restored. Wholeness in your intimacy with Jesus, wholeness in you, wholeness in your intimacy with your husband, and wholeness in your household; it all begins with you—when you surrender to Jesus, obey, and believe; you must believe.

Encouragement

The Bride:
Thus saith the Lord; If ye can break My covenant of the day, and My covenant of the night, and that there should not be day and night in their season; Then may also My covenant be broken with David My servant, that he should not have a son to reign upon his throne; and with the Levites the priests, My ministers. As the host of heaven cannot be numbered, neither the sand of the sea measured: so will I multiply the seed of David My servant, and the Levites that minister unto Me. Considerest thou not what this people have spoken, saying, The two families which the Lord hath chosen, He hath even cast them off? Thus they have despised My people, that they should be no more a nation before them. Thus saith the Lord; If My covenant be not with day and night, and if I have not appointed the ordinances of the heaven and earth; Then will I cast away the seed of Jacob, and David My servant, so that I will not take any of his seed to be rulers over the seed of Abraham, Isaac, and Jacob; for I will cause their captivity to return, and have mercy on them.

The wife: For Mine eyes are upon all their ways: they are not hid from My face, neither is their iniquity hid from Mine eyes.

Amen (truly, so be it).

www.ingramcontent.com/pod-product-compliance
Lightning Source LLC
Chambersburg PA
CBHW070552300426
44113CB00011B/1876